Activity Book FOR GIRLS
AGES 8-12

90 FUN ACTIVITIES

THIS BOOK BELONGS TO

_ _ _ _ _ _ _ _ _ _ _ _ _ _ _ _ _ _ _

_ _ _ _ _ _ _ _ _ _ _ _ _ _ _ _ _ _ _

Welcome

to your very own

Activity Book For Girls Ages 8-12!

This book is packed with 90 fun and fabulous activities just for you. Whether you love coloring, drawing, solving puzzles, or tackling math challenges, there's something here to spark your creativity and keep you entertained. Get ready to dive into a world of imagination and adventure. Remember, there's no limit to what you can create and discover.

Have fun and let your imagination soar!

ALL ABOUT ME!

I AM

YEARS OLD

WHAT I LIKE TO DO

MY NAME IS

Mi FAVORITE ANIMAL IS ...

MY FAVORITE COLOR IS ...

MY FAVORITE FOOD IS ..

When i grow up, i want to be...

PYRAMID MAZE

Help the archaeologists find the room holding precious pharaoh jewels.

Beware of the Lurking mummies

SHADOW MATCHING #1

Can you find the correct Shadow?

GLAM UP!

Show off your makeup skills and give this girl a stunning makeover that highlights her beauty! Have fun and let your creativity shine!

AXOLOTL

- **Mexican Heritage:** Axolotls are native to lakes around Mexico City, especially Lake Xochimilco. Their name comes from the Aztec word "atl" (water) and "xolotl" (monster).

- **Size and Appearance:** Axolotls can grow up to 12 inches (30 cm) long, though they are often shorter. They have small legs and feet, a long tail, and a fin that runs from head to tail.

- **Regeneration Ability:** Axolotls can regenerate almost any part of their body, including limbs, tail, heart, and even parts of their brain, making them a marvel in the animal kingdom

- **Variety of Colors:** While wild axolotls are usually brown or black, captive ones can be found in a variety of colors, including white, pink, and gold.

- **No Need for Eyelids:** Axolotls don't have eyelids, so their eyes are always open, even when they are resting.

- **Long Lives:** Axolotls can live up to 15 years in captivity with proper care, providing a long-term companionship for their owners.

- **Diet:** Axolotls eat fish, mollusks, insects, and even other axolotls. In captivity, they can be fed with specially prepared food or live prey like worms.

- **Night Owls:** Axolotls are nocturnal, meaning they are most active at night. They prefer dim light and often hide during the day.

WHAT IS THIS UNICORN SAYING?

HOW OLD AM I?

Read the descriptions of the kids to find out their ages.
Write the kids' ages below.

*Emma is 4 years older than Liam.

*Olivia is the same age as Ashley.

*Noah is 3 years older than Emma.

*Liam is 10 years old.

*Ashley is 2 years younger than Noah, and 1 year older than Mia.

Liam	Emma	Olivia

Liam	Emma	Olivia

FASHION WORD SEARCH

Try to find all the hidden words in the word search puzzle below.
Words can be found forwards, backwards, diagonally, up, or down.

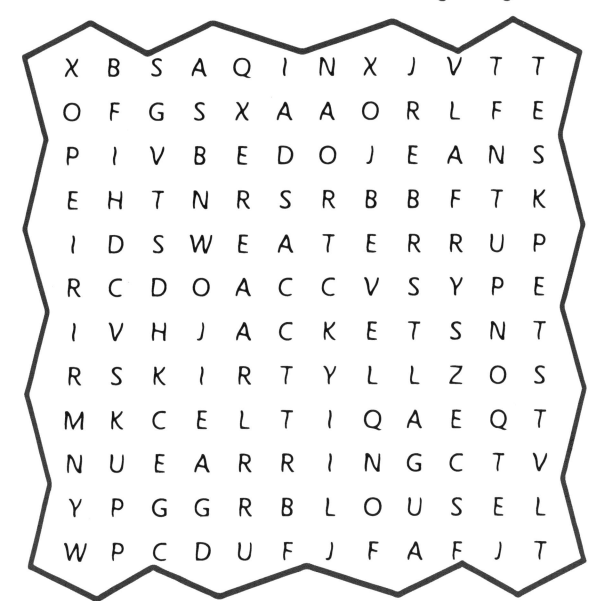

```
X  B  S  A  Q  I  N  X  J  V  T  T
O  F  G  S  X  A  A  O  R  L  F  E
P  I  V  B  E  D  O  J  E  A  N  S
E  H  T  N  R  S  R  B  B  F  T  K
I  D  S  W  E  A  T  E  R  R  U  P
R  C  D  O  A  C  C  V  S  Y  P  E
I  V  H  J  A  C  K  E  T  S  N  T
R  S  K  I  R  T  Y  L  L  Z  O  S
M  K  C  E  L  T  I  Q  A  E  Q  T
N  U  E  A  R  R  I  N  G  C  T  V
Y  P  G  G  R  B  L  O  U  S  E  L
W  P  C  D  U  F  J  F  A  F  J  T
```

Words to Finds

Dress	Jacket	Necklace
Skirt	Shoes	Earring
Blouse	Scarf	Belt
Jeans	Bracelet	Sweater

SPOT THE DIFFERENCES #1

Can you find the 7 differences in these two pictures?

GRANDPA'S BERRY PUZZLE

Figure out the age and favorite fruit of each of the granddaughters.

Amelie, Beatrice, Claire, and Donna went to visit their grandpa, who took them to enjoy the red fruits in the garden:

Fruits: Raspberries, Strawberries, Blueberries, Blackberries

Clues:

- They are 9, 11, 12, and 14 years old, and each girl has a different favorite fruit.

- Donna likes blackberries.

- The girl who likes blueberries is two years older than Beatrice.

- Beatrice doesn't like raspberries.

- Amelie is 12 years old.

Names	Fruit	Age
Amelie		
Beatrice		
Claire		
Donna		

JOKES DECODING #1

Can you crack the code and unravel the joke?

a	b	c	d	e	f	g	h	i	j	k	l	m
1	2	3	4	5	6	7	8	9	10	11	12	13

n	o	p	q	r	s	t	u	v	w	x	y	z
14	15	16	17	18	19	20	21	22	23	24	25	26

Why couldn't the bicycle stand up by itself?

9	20		23	1	19		20	23	15		20	25	18	5	4

What do rabbits say before they eat?

12	5	20	20	21	3	5		16	18	1	25

What did the zero say to the eight?

14	9	3	5		2	5	12	20

What kind of doctor does a duck visit?

1		4	21	3	11	20	15	18

14

HOW TO DRAW: AXOLOTL

Get ready to draw an adorable axolotl step by step! Follow these easy instructions and soon you'll have your very own cute axolotl drawing. Grab your pencils and let's get started!

PRACTICE

CONNECT THE DOTS #1

Join the dots to reveal the picture

WORD LADDER ADVENTURE #1

Transform the starting word into the ending word by changing one letter at a time. Each intermediate step must be a valid word. You can use the clues provided to help you figure out each intermediate word.

The nickname for dinosaur. **D I N O**

To go out to eat.

It belongs to me so it is __

A fancy word for brain.

To tie or fasten something.

A type of animal with wings. **B I R D**

DESIGN YOUR DREAM DRESS!

Unleash your inner fashion designer and create a one-of-a-kind dress that shows off your unique style.

18

GUESS THE FASHION BRAND #1

Put your fashion knowledge to the test as you decipher the clues and uncover the names of famous fashion and retail brands

1. This brand was founded by a French designer in 1946.

2. It's famous for its "New Look" that revolutionized women's fashion in the 1950s.

3. The brand's iconic perfume is called "Miss ____".

4. Known for its luxurious dresses often seen on red carpets.

5. The logo features a simple and elegant "CD".

Brand Name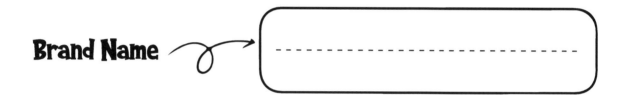

1. An Italian luxury brand founded in 1921 by Guccio Gucci.

2. Known for its green and red striped webbing.

3. The logo features double "G"s.

4. Famous for its stylish and high-quality leather goods.

5. Popular for its bold and extravagant designs.

Brand Name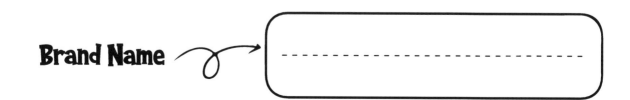

FASHION CROSSWORDS

Across

3. One-piece garment worn by females
6. Protective garment worn over clothes while cooking
7. Fastener that fits through a hole
8. Worn on the feet to keep them warm or for comfort
10. Covers the head

Down

1. Clothing fastener with teeth
2. Worn around the waist to hold up pants
4. Pants that leave your legs bare
5. Casual pants made of denim fabric
9. Outerwear worn for warmth in cold weather, longer than jacket

MISSING DIGITS

Fill in the missing numbers to make each addition and subtraction equation true.

1.
$$
\begin{array}{r}
\_\_,345 \\
+\ 12,\_\_3 \\
\hline
34,568
\end{array}
$$

2.
$$
\begin{array}{r}
6\_,78\_ \\
+\ 2\_,913 \\
\hline
90,703
\end{array}
$$

3.
$$
\begin{array}{r}
45,\_01 \\
-\ 2\_,349 \\
\hline
20,\_52
\end{array}
$$

4.
$$
\begin{array}{r}
9\_,432 \\
-\ \_8,210 \\
\hline
45,\_22
\end{array}
$$

5.
$$
\begin{array}{r}
8\_,234 \\
+\ 3\_,911 \\
\hline
12\_,145
\end{array}
$$

6.
$$
\begin{array}{r}
\_\_,789 \\
-\ 3\_,451 \\
\hline
24,338
\end{array}
$$

7.
$$
\begin{array}{r}
7\_,109 \\
+\ 1\_,884 \\
\hline
92,\_93
\end{array}
$$

8.
$$
\begin{array}{r}
54,\_\_7 \\
-\ 12,\_\_6 \\
\hline
41,871
\end{array}
$$

9.
$$
\begin{array}{r}
6\_,543 \\
+\ 3\_,987 \\
\hline
100,530
\end{array}
$$

THE KNIGHT'S QUEST

Can you help the knight solve the maze and save the princess?

EASTER EGG

Unleash your creativity and decorate the Easter egg in your own unique style!

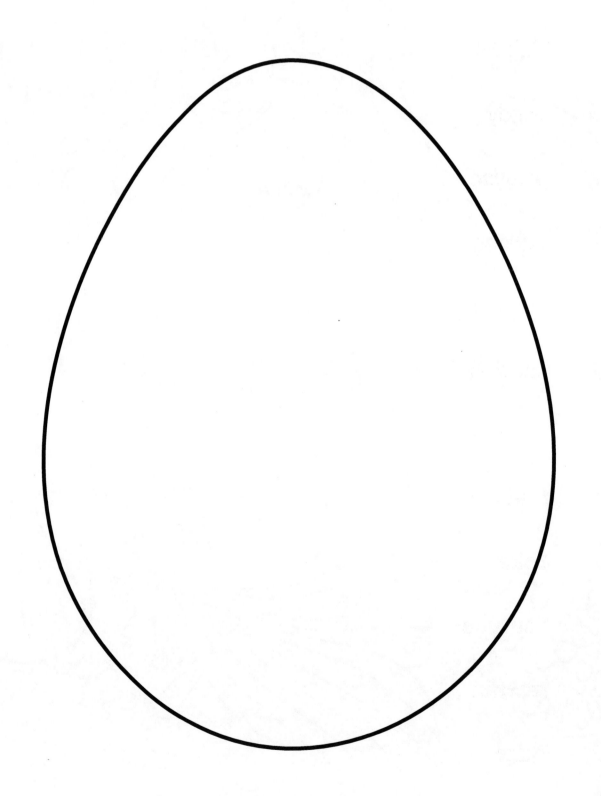

THiS OR THAT!

Make your choice and stand by it!

○   Dogs   Or   Cats   ○

○   Pink Hair   Or   Blue Hair   ○

○   Candy   Or   Chocolate   ○

○   Sunrise   Or   Sunset   ○

○   Talking   Or   Texting   ○

○   Singing   Or   Dancing   ○

○   Read A Book   Or   Watch A Movie   ○

○   Sweats   Or   Dresses   ○

○   Salty   Or   Sweet   ○

○   Coke   Or   Pepsi   ○

○   Youtube   Or   Tiktok   ○

○   Netflix   Or   Games   ○

○   Pizza   Or   Burgers   ○

DINNER PARTY SEATING PUZZLE

Can you correctly place the six people around the table?

During a dinner party, three couples sat around a table with the following rules:

1. No man sat next to another man.

2. No man sat next to or across from his wife.

3. Mr. Smith did not sit next to or across from Mrs. Johnson.

4. Mrs. Johnson likes to chat with Mrs. Brown, who sat next to her.

5. Mr. Brown did not sit next to the window.

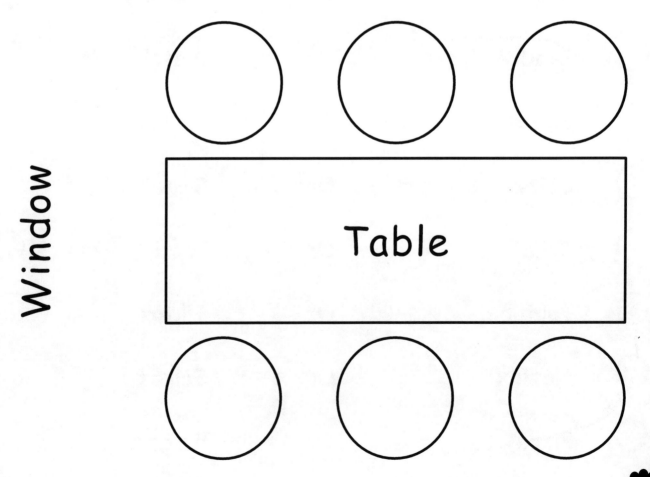

DESIGN YOUR DREAM HANDBAG!

Create your own unique handbag. Unleash your inner fashionista and let your creativity shine!

SHADOW MATCHING #2

Can you find the correct Shadow?

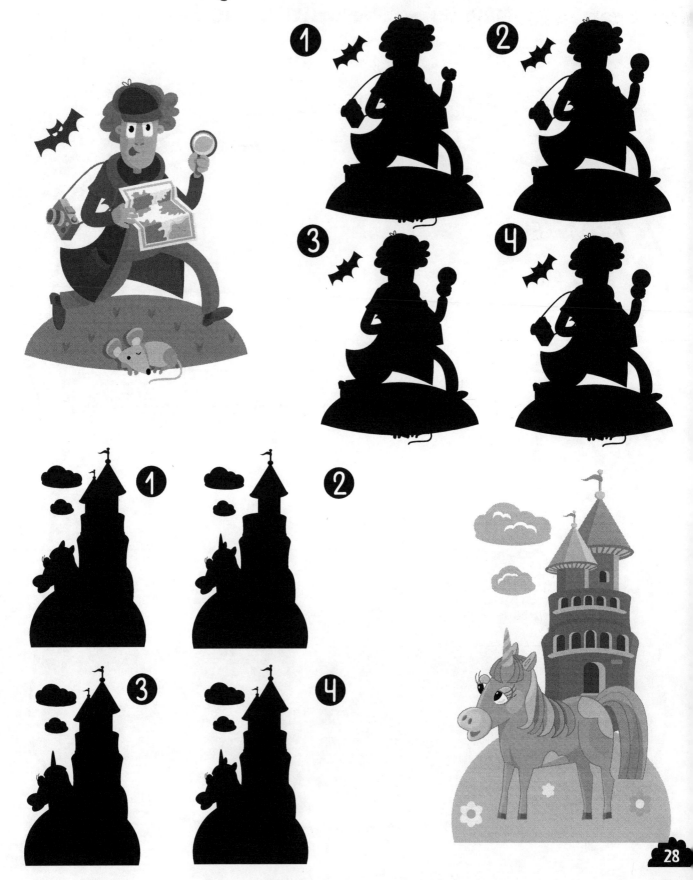

ADVENTURE WORD SEARCH

Try to find all the hidden words in the word search puzzle below.
Words can be found forwards, backwards, diagonally, up, or down.

```
D  C  O  K  T  Y  C  E  O  Q  R  K
Y  I  Y  N  B  Q  C  M  K  A  T  T
Y  F  B  D  E  S  E  R  T  E  C  R
M  E  G  M  B  X  X  I  R  Q  F  E
D  H  C  O  K  X  P  Q  Y  G  V  A
I  A  J  U  N  G  L  E  M  C  B  S
B  S  I  N  L  I  O  R  C  C  S  U
H  R  L  T  R  C  R  I  I  A  Q  R
E  S  T  A  A  S  E  K  P  V  M  E
J  P  F  I  N  M  R  M  Q  E  E  P
R  A  I  N  H  D  O  X  I  A  B  R
S  M  J  V  O  C  E  A  N  R  J  A
```

Words to Finds

Explorer	Mountain	River
Treasure	Desert	Island
Compass	Ocean	Safari
Jungle	Cave	Camp

29

SUDOKU #1

Medium 1

6				4	
			3		
	3	5	1		
1				5	3
		4	5		
5					

Medium 2

5	3		6		4
	6		1	4	
4		5			2
1	5		4		6

Medium 3

1		4			5
	5		4	1	
	4				
		2			4
	3		2		
					1

Medium 4

			4		
	4				1
	2				
1			3		
4		2	5		
	5			4	2

SPACE EXPLORATION

- **First Human in Space:** Yuri Gagarin, a Russian astronaut, was the first person to travel into space on April 12, 1961.

- **First American Woman in Space:** Sally Ride became the first American woman to travel into space On June 18, 1983.

- On Venus, a year is 225 Earth days, but a day is 243 Earth days. This means a single day on Venus is longer than its entire year!

- About 1.3 million Earths could fit inside the Sun, which is considered an average-sized star in our galaxy.

- Space junk includes any human-made objects orbiting Earth that no longer serve a purpose. There are about 500,000 pieces, from rocket fragments and satellites to tools dropped during ISS construction.

- **Stars in the Universe:** There are more stars in the universe than grains of sand on all Earth's beaches. That's at least a billion trillion stars!

- **Solar Eclipses:** Solar eclipses happen when the Moon moves between Earth and the Sun, blocking the Sun from view. They don't happen often because the Moon's orbit is a bit wobbly.

- **Black Holes:** Black holes are super powerful and form when huge stars collapse. Their gravity is so strong that even light can't escape! Don't worry, the nearest one is thousands of light-years away.

SPOT THE DIFFERENCES #2

Can you find the 9 differences in these two pictures?

HOW TO DRAW: MUSHROOM

Get ready to draw an adorable Mushroom step by step! Follow These easy instructions and soon you'll have your very own cute Mushroom drawing. Grab your pencils and let's get started!

34

NAME THESE CATS

Look at each cat and come up with a fun name that matches its unique appearance. Be creative and give each cat a special name!

JOKES DECODING #2

Can you crack the code and unravel the joke?

a	b	c	d	e	f	g	h	i	j	k	l	m
1	2	3	4	5	6	7	8	9	10	11	12	13

n	o	p	q	r	s	t	u	v	w	x	y	z
14	15	16	17	18	19	20	21	22	23	24	25	26

What kind of fish is the most valuable?

7	15	12	4	6	9	19	8

How do the oceans say hello to each other?

20	8	5	25		23	1	22	5

What do you call a golden retriever at the beach?

1	8	15	20		4	15	7

Where do sharks go on vacation?

6	9	14	12	1	14	4

36

SMOOTHIE CREATION

Blend up a delicious and refreshing smoothie! Then,
decorate your glass to show off your tasty creation.

Name of the smoothie: _

Ingredients Needed:

_ _

_ _

_ _

_ _

_ _

_ _

_ _

_ _

_ _

_ _

DRAWING ACTIVITIES

Show off your drawing talents and finish the other half of the picture!

MiXED UP CROWNS

Use the clues and grid to solve the puzzle.

	Red	Blue	Green	Yellow	Purple
George					
Henry					
Richard					
Louis					
John					

CLUES:

Five kings have mixed up their crowns. Help sort them out.

1. King George's crown is not green or red.

2. King Richard's crown is red or yellow.

3. King John's crown is not blue or purple.

4. The purple crown does not belong to Henry or George.

5. If the kings stand in alphabetical order, the red crown belongs to the king who is last.

6. King Henry's crown matches his boots, which are the color of water.

39

MOTHER EARTH

Write a special thank you note to show how much you appreciate our Planet Earth!

WORD LADDER ADVENTURE #2

Transform the starting word into the ending word by changing one letter at a time. Each intermediate step must be a valid word. You can use the clues provided to help you figure out each intermediate word.

Something you play. **G A M E**

A very strong wind.

A bundle of hay.

A round object you play sports with.

A hollow metal object that chimes

Something that holds up your pants.

When ice turns into water. **M E L T**

SPACE CROSSWORDS

Across

1. The force that keeps planets in orbit around the Sun.

4. A small, rocky planet closest to the Sun, named after the Roman messenger god.

6. The fourth planet from the Sun, often called the 'Red Planet'.

8. The _____ Galaxy is the large spiral of stars that includes our solar system.

9. The third planet from the Sun is called _____.

Down

2. The study of stars, planets, and space.

3. The closest star to Earth.

4. The shiny object that orbits Earth and reflects sunlight at night.

5. The largest planet in our solar system, with a big red spot.

7. A giant ball of gas that shines brightly in the night sky.

ARRANGE THE CARS

Can you figure out the order of the cars?

Sophia has five cars of different colors: one blue, one gray, one yellow, one red, and one green. She notices the following:

- The gray car is next to the green car.

- There are two cars between the red car and the blue car.

- The red car is not at either end.

- The yellow car is to the left of the gray car, but there is another car between them.

FIND THE SPACESHIP

Can you help the astronaut find his missing spaceship so he can return home?

DESiGN YOUR DREAM SHOES!

Let your imagination run wild and create your own unique shoes
Show off your style and creativity!

CONNECT THE DOTS #2

Join the dots to reveal the picture

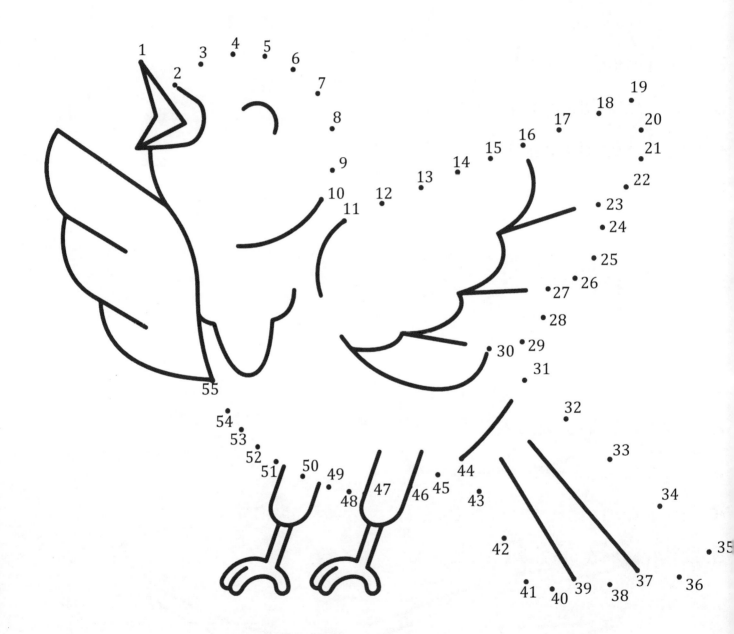

GUESS THE FASHION BRAND #2

Put your fashion knowledge to the test as you decipher the clues and uncover the names of famous fashion and retail brands

1. Founded by a famous French designer known for her timeless style in 1910.

2. This brand's little black dress and tweed suits are legendary.

3. The brand's logo features two interlocking "C"s.

4. Known for the perfume "No. 5".

5. Famous for its quilted handbags and classic designs.

Brand Name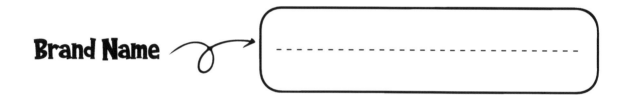

1. Founded in Milan, Italy, in 1913 by Mario Prada.

2. Known for its minimalist and sophisticated designs.

3. The brand is famous for its nylon bags.

4. The logo features a triangle with the brand's name.

5. Often seen on the runways with sleek and modern fashion.

Brand Name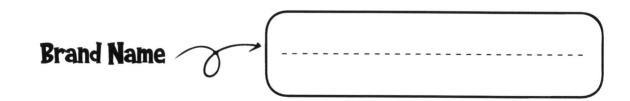

MAGICAL DREAM

**What do you think this girl is dreaming about?
Draw or write her dream!**

SUDOKU #2

Medium 5

		5			2
			6		
	1			3	
		3			1
	2			4	
4					

Medium 6

					2
	6			1	
1					4
	4				
4		2			5
	5		2	4	

Medium 7

		1		4	
	4		1		
		2		5	
5					
	6		2		
					3

Medium 8

		1		5	
5					1
6					3
			6		
		3		2	
	4				

ANIMALS WORD SEARCH

Try to find all the hidden words in the word search puzzle below.
Words can be found forwards, backwards, diagonally, up, or down

```
T P E T K A N G A R O O
D W G M S N R Z U I G N
J O P D Y S Y Z C D J I
A U L E O P A R D Y F F
H W K P E N G U I N E L
L X O H H G O R I L L A
J T A Q T I G E R J E M
V F L T A R N O G K P I
C P A N D A Z M J A H N
I T J J U F M B K O A G
G R U I K F C I K Y N O
D Q Z T Z E B R A D T M
```

Words to Finds

Elephant

Giraffe

Kangaroo

Dolphin

Penguin

Tiger

Zebra

Gorilla

Panda

Koala

Leopard

Flamingo

52

HOW TO DRAW: RABBIT

Get ready to draw an adorable Rabbit step by step! Follow These easy instructions and soon you'll have your very own cute Rabbit drawing. Grab your pencils and let's get started!

START

PRACTICE

SLOTHS

- Sloths are known for being incredibly slow animals. They move at a very leisurely pace, and their slow movements help them conserve energy.

- Sloths are famous for their long naps. They can sleep for up to 15 to 20 hours a day! They are most active at night.

- There are two main types of sloths: three-toed and two-toed. Despite their names, both types actually have three toes on their hind limbs. The difference lies in the number of fingers on their front limbs.

- Sloths are speedy swimmers, they are 3 times faster in water than they are on land and they can hold their breath for an impressive 40 minutes. Their preferred swimming style is the backstroke.

- Upside down is the best way round for a sloth. An average sloth spends 90% of its life hanging upside down, achievable as they can breathe normally in this position

- Female sloths give birth to one baby a year after a pregnancy period of 6 to 10 months. The baby sticks with the mother for a bonding period of six months in which the offspring learn and develop.

- Sloths are famous for their unique bathroom routine. They have a "once-a-week" policy for relieving themselves, and during this event, they can lose up to a third of their body weight!

IN 20 YEARS...

Envision yourself two decades into the future. What will your life be like? Fill in the sentences with the wonderful things that will make your life uniquely amazing.

By: _____

In 20 years, I will be _____ years old

I will live in _____

I will be working as _____

I will have a pet _____

I will still love to _____

I will have visited _____ countries.

I will have achieved _____

my favorite place to be will be _____

my best friend will be _____

my favorite food will still be _____

I will drive a _____

55

WRITE A SHORT STORY

You and your best friend discover an old map in your attic that leads to hidden treasure.

Describe your adventure to find it.

ACCESSORIZE THIS HAND

Time to show off your style! Accessorize this hand however you like. Draw rings, bracelets, nail art, or anything else that makes it unique and fabulous. Let your creativity shine!

SHADOW MATCHING #3

Can you find the correct Shadow?

JOKES DECODING #3

Can you crack the code and unravel the joke?

a	b	c	d	e	f	g	h	i	j	k	l	m
1	2	3	4	5	6	7	8	9	10	11	12	13

n	o	p	q	r	s	t	u	v	w	x	y	z
14	15	16	17	18	19	20	21	22	23	24	25	26

What did the bored goat say?

13	5	8	8	8

What does a dinosaur call a porcupine?

1	20	15	15	20	8	2	18	21	19	8

What's as big as a dinosaur but weighs nothing?

9	20	19		19	8	1	4	15	23

What did the little corn say to the mama corn?

23	8	5	18	5		9	19		16	15	16		3	15	18	14

WHO SITS WHERE?

Can you arrange the guests correctly around the table?

Scenario:

Around a round table, Roger is immediately to the left of Sam. Lily is neither next to Emma nor immediately to the right of John, but she is across from Rachel. There are only six people at the table.

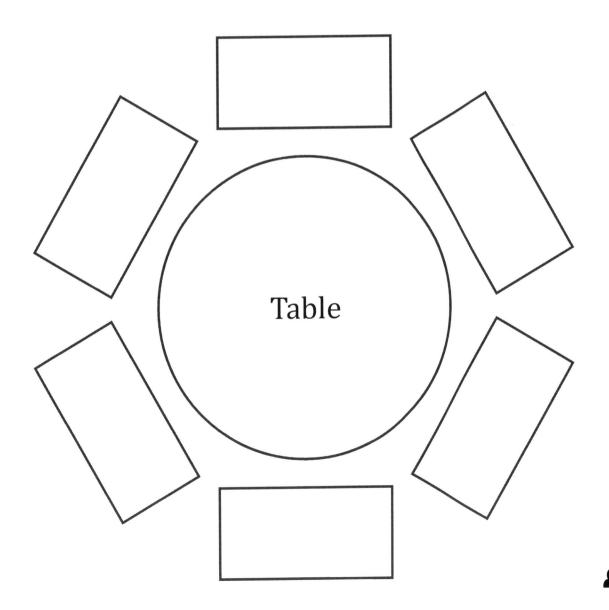

Table

SPOT THE DIFFERENCES #3

Can you find the 8 differences in these two pictures?

BAKING CROSSWORDS

Across

2. Protein found in wheat, barley, rye. It acts like a binder, while being stretchy.

5. Fine powder used to make cakes fluffy.

7. When you whip egg whites, they can what?

8. Tool used to mix batter.

9. Sweet, liquid flavoring often used in baking.

10. Powdery ingredient that helps dough rise.

Down

1. Softened butter and sugar beaten together.

3. Circular metal pan for baking cakes.

4. Mixing cream and chocolate will make what?

6. Thin, flat tool for lifting cookies off a tray.

MONSTER FRIENDS

Help Pookie the monster find his friend Wiggles! Solve the math maze by coloring only the circles that have even numbers inside.

54 x 5 =

37 x 3 =

85 x 7 =

53 x 9 =

26 x 6 =

86 x 9 =

48 x 2 =

27 x 7 =

87 x 3 =

79 x 5 =

37 x 8 =

88 x 7 =

75 x 6 =

64 x 4 =

98 x 3 =

96 x 5 =

47 x 9 =

GUESS THE FASHION BRAND #3

Put your fashion knowledge to the test as you decipher the clues and uncover the names of famous fashion and retail brands

1. A French luxury brand founded in 1854.

2. Famous for its monogram "LV" logo.

3. Known for its high-quality leather goods and luggage.

4. The brand's iconic pattern includes flowers and quatrefoils.

5. Often associated with elegant travel accessories and handbags.

Brand Name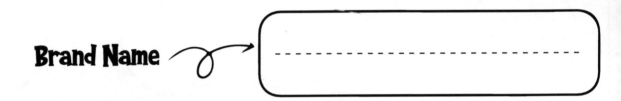

1. Founded by an American designer in 1967.

2. Famous for its polo shirts with a horse and rider logo.

3. The brand's collections include preppy and classic American styles.

4. Known for its high-end and affordable lines, including Polo Ralph Lauren.

5. Has a famous flagship store on Madison Avenue in New York City.

Brand Name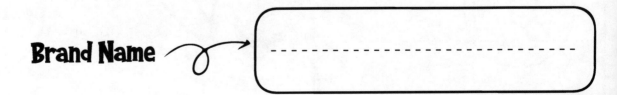

SHOPPING ADVENTURE PUZZLE

Sam, Jack, Jim and Mary went to the store. They each had a Different amount of money and bought something different. Use the Clues to figure out how much money they had and what they bought

	Sam	Jack	Jm	Mary	Toy	Candy	Book	Game
$3.00								
$5.00								
$8.00								
$10.00								
Toy				
Candy				
Book				
Game				

Write your answers below

Name	Money	Bought

CLUES:

1. The game was the most expensive item

2. Jack isn't allowed to eat candy

3. Jm had three dollars less than Mary

4. Sam did not buy the toy or the game

5. The book costs $5.00

SPOOKY CEMETERY MAZE!

Can you find your way out of the spooky cemetery before the zombies wake up?

START

FINISH

WORD LADDER ADVENTURE #3

Transform the starting word into the ending word by changing one letter at a time. Each intermediate step must be a valid word. You can use the clues provided to help you figure out each intermediate word.

A synonym for big or massive.

H U G E

A sport where someone slides down an icy track.

To get something to come to you.

To make an illness go away.

To love or help someone.

Plural of car.

Body parts that you hear from.

E A R S

WHAT'S GROWING ON THIS TREE?

Your answer can be realistic or imaginative.

CONNECT THE DOTS #3

Join the dots to reveal the picture

FANTASY WORD SEARCH

Try to find all the hidden words in the word search puzzle below. Words can be found forwards, backwards, diagonally, up, or down.

```
C A Y J G V X E K W X V
J A T H F G O B L I N V
L K B E A A N M N Z G R
K T L B N K I E K A V E
B B O V F C O R N R Q S
L L Z J Y H H M Y D M C
Z H L D P B M A J K E Y
L A G R I F F I N L L P
F X E A L N I D T T F U
K N I G H T H S M X E C
I U R O P M A G I C P D
N W U N I C O R N T Y Q
```

Words to Finds

Dragon   Goblin   Knight
Unicorn   Mermaid   Magic
Fairy   Phoenix   Enchanted
Wizard   Castle   Griffin

BLOSSOMED FLOWERS

Color the next drawing and discover how beautiful they are!

73

CREATE YOUR OWN FLAG!

Design a flag that hat represents you! Use your favorite colors, symbols, and patterns to make it unique and special.

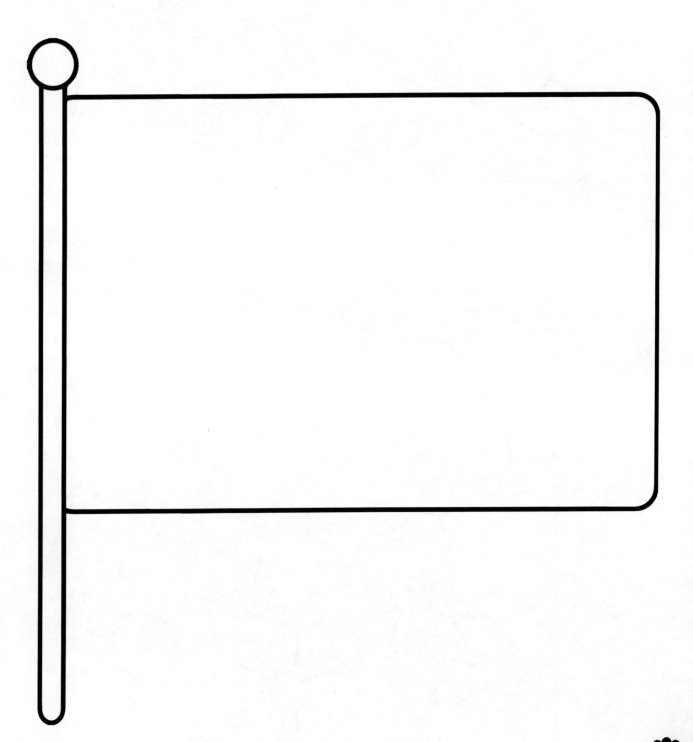

MELODY'S COLORING CHALLENGE

Melody has colored each square in this grid yellow, red, or green. Can you figure out her coloring pattern knowing that:

- There are three squares of each color.

- There are two green squares in the second row and no yellow.

- There are two yellow squares in the third row and no green.

- There are two red squares in the first column and no green.

- There are two yellow squares in the third column and no red

SUDOKU #3

Hard 1

		4			2
1				6	
					1
5			2	4	
4					
	3	5			4

Hard 2

	1				
2		6			1
1					5
	4			3	
					4
	2		5	1	

Hard 3

	1				
2		4	5		
		6		1	
	2		4		
	4		5		3
				4	

Hard 4

				5	
4			6		3
5					1
		3		6	
3					
	2	4		3	

PYRAMID ADDITION

Can you determine the top number of each pyramid?
Add each pair of blocks together to find the number that appears
in the block directly above them.

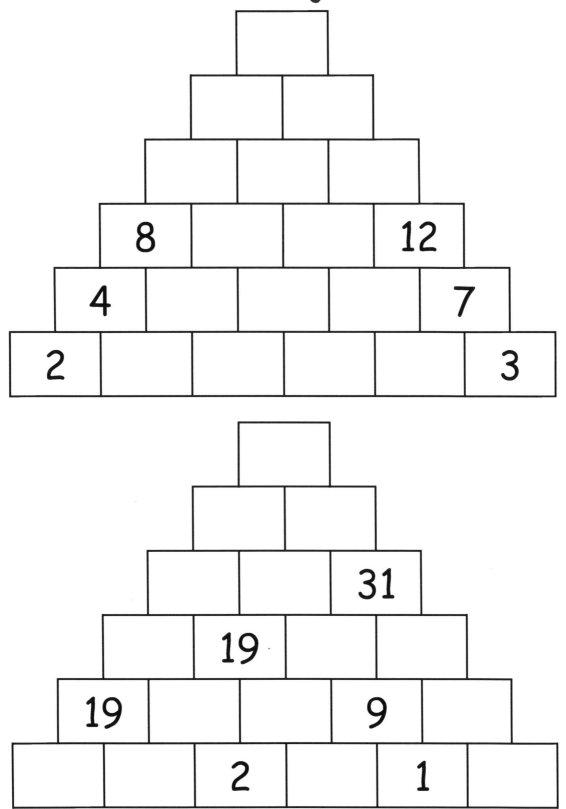

HUMAN BODY #1

- **Amazing Brain:** your brain is like a supercomputer. It has about 86 billion nerve cells and can process information faster than any computer.

- **Heart Power:** Your heart beats about 100,000 times a day, pumping blood to every part of your body. It's only the size of your fist but works non-stop!

- **Bone Count:** Babies are born with around 270 bones, but adults have only 206 because some bones fuse together as we grow.

- **Super Skin:** Your skin is the largest organ in your body. It protects you, helps regulate body temperature, and lets you feel touch.

- **Fast Nails:** Fingernails grow faster than toenails. On average, your fingernails grow about 0.1 inches (2.5 mm) per month.

- **Unique Prints:** Your fingerprints are unique to you. No one else in the world has the same fingerprint pattern, even identical twins!

- **Quick Blinks:** You blink about 15-20 times per minute, which keeps your eyes moist and free of dust. That's about 1,200 blinks an hour!

- **Blood Journey:** Blood travels through your body's 60,000 miles of blood vessels, which is enough to circle the Earth more than twice!

- **Tiny Hairs:** Your ears have tiny hairs that help you hear. These hairs pick up sound vibrations and send signals to your brain.

DESIGN YOUR DREAM PACK

Unleash your creativity and design a backpack that's uniquely you!

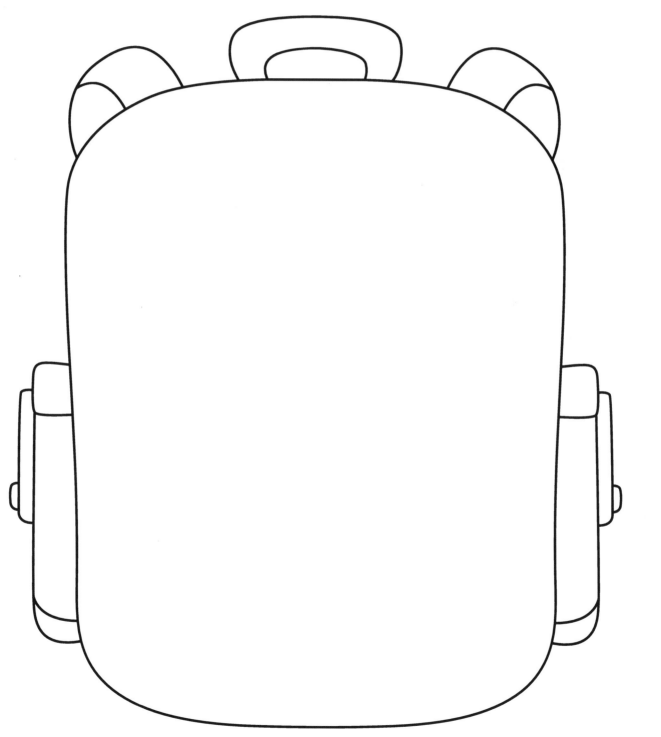

NUMBER ARROW CHALLENGE

Arrange the following numbers following this rule:
"An arrow always points from a smaller number to
a larger number."

1,0001	1,0011	1,01	1,011
1,1	1,10001	1,101	

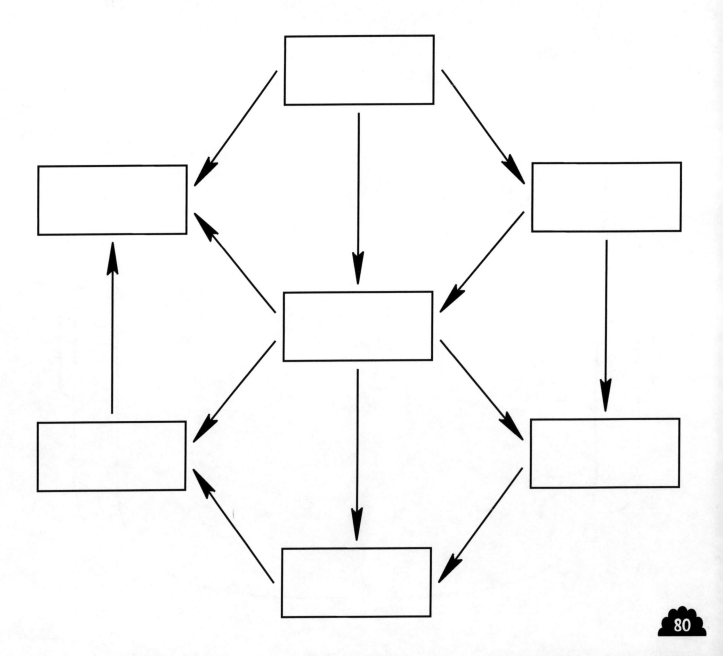

GROW KINDNESS NOT HATE!

Write some kind things you've done for yourself or others in the bubbles below

SPOT THE DIFFERENCES #4

Can you find the 7 differences in these two pictures?

GRANDMA'S JAM JARS

My grandma makes delicious jams. There are three flavors: blueberry, peach, and raspberry. She has three jars: one large, one medium, and one small.

- The large jar doesn't have blueberry jam.

- The small jar doesn't have peach jam

Can you match each jar with the jam it contains?

SCISSOR SEARCH

Help this little fashionista find her way through the maze to recover her favorite scissor!

GUESS THE FASHION BRAND #4

Put your fashion knowledge to the test as you decipher the clues and uncover the names of famous fashion and retail brands

1. A British luxury brand founded in 1856 by Thomas Burberry.

2. Known for its iconic trench coats and checkered pattern.

3. The logo features a knight on horseback.

4. Famous for its classic and timeless designs.

5. Often associated with British heritage and style.

Brand Name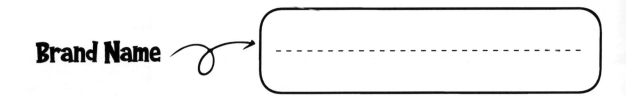

1. An American brand founded in 1964, originally known as Blue Ribbon Sports.

2. The logo is a simple "Swoosh" symbol.

3. Famous for its athletic shoes and sportswear.

4. The brand's slogan is "Just Do It".

5. Known for collaborations with athletes and popular sneaker lines.

Brand Name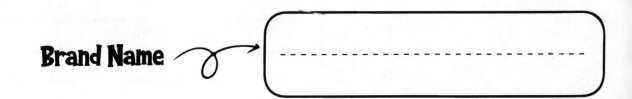

INSECTS CROSSWORDS

Across

2. Small, black insects that march in lines.

5. Insects that build intricate silk homes.

6. These insects have long, thin bodies and are often found near water.

8. Winged insects that chirp at night.

9. Caterpillar becomes this.

Down

1. Nighttime cousins of butterflies and are attracted to light sources at night.

3. Glowing bugs at night.

4. Expert jumpers in the grass.

7. Six-legged crawlers.

9. Small, buzzing insect that makes honey.

SHADOW MATCHING #4

Can you find the correct Shadow?

HUMAN BODY #2

- **Lively Liver:** Your liver has over 500 functions, including filtering toxins from your blood, producing bile for digestion, and storing vitamins and energy.

- **Tasty Taste Buds:** You have about 10,000 taste buds on your tongue that help you taste sweet, sour, salty, bitter, and umami (savory) flavors.

- **Fast Feet:** Your feet have 26 bones, 33 joints, and more than 100 muscles, tendons, and ligaments each. They work together to help you walk, run, and balance.

- **Super Speed:** Nerve impulses in your body travel at speeds of up to 250 miles per hour, allowing you to react quickly to things around you.

- **Growing Hair:** Your hair grows about half an inch (1.25 cm) per month. That's about 6 inches (15 cm) a year!

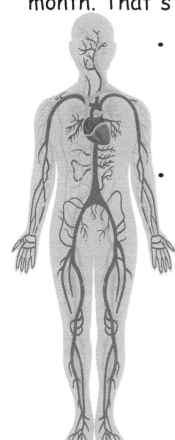

- **Sensitive Fingertips:** Your fingertips are extremely sensitive because they have a high concentration of nerve endings, helping you feel textures and temperatures.

- **Muscle Count:** Your body has more than 600 muscles. They help you move, lift things, and maintain your posture.

- **Smell Memory:** Your sense of smell is closely linked to your memory. Scents can trigger vivid memories and emotions.

- **Flexible Spine:** Your spine is made up of 33 vertebrae. It's incredibly flexible, allowing you to bend, twist, and move in many directions.

FOOD WORD SEARCH

Try to find all the hidden words in the word search puzzle below.
Words can be found forwards, backwards, diagonally, up, or down.

```
J  B  T  K  X  P  W  A  R  D  W  Y
F  J  Q  R  W  M  T  B  A  A  X  M
F  F  H  T  Z  S  R  L  T  E  Q  U
S  H  C  B  A  J  A  I  P  S  N  O
T  X  Z  P  U  S  U  R  E  U  E  Y
Q  I  X  W  A  R  O  Q  J  S  S  T
Y  R  D  M  F  N  G  U  E  H  Q  D
T  A  L  P  F  L  C  E  P  I  F  X
D  Q  C  I  Z  B  H  A  R  E  I  T
D  B  F  Z  I  C  O  O  K  I  E  H
O  Z  W  Z  I  C  E  C  R  E  A  M
C  A  S  A  N  D  W  I  C  H  V  Y
```

Words to Finds

Pizza	Sushi	Soup
Burger	Ice Cream	Fruit
Salad	Pancake	Cookie
Pasta	Sandwich	Cheese

ALLIGATOR SNACK TIME!

What do you think this alligator is about to munch on? Draw it!

SOLUTIONS

Pyramid Maze

How Old Am I?

Liam: 10

Emma: 14

Olivia: 15

Ashley: 15

Noah: 17

Mia: 14

Fashion Word Search

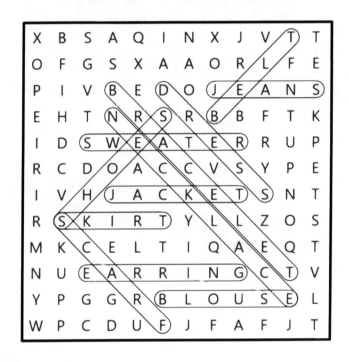

Grandpa's Berry Puzzle

Names	Fruit	Age
Amelie	Raspberries	12
Beatrice	Strawberries	9
Claire	Blueberries	11
Donna	Blackberries	14

Jokes Decoding #1

Q: Why couldn't the bicycle stand up by itself?
A: It was two tyred!
Q: What do rabbits say before they eat?
A: Lettuce pray
Q: What did the zero say to the eight?
A: Nice belt!
Q: What kind of doctor does a duck visit?
A: A Ducktor

Word Ladder Adventure #1

DINO
DINE
MINE
MIND
BIND
BIRD

Guess the Fashion Brand #1

1. Dior
2. Gucci

Fashion Crosswords

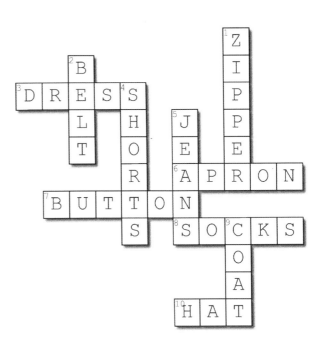

Missing Digits

1. 22,345 + 12,223 = 34,568
2. 63,782 + 27,913 = 90,703
3. 45,601 – 25,349 = 20,252
4. 91,432 – 46,210 = 45,222
5. 82,234 + 39,911 = 122,145
6. 64,789 – 20,451 = 44,338
7. 72,109 + 20,884 = 92,993
8. 54,307 – 12,436 = 41,871
9. 65,543 + 35,987 = 100,530

The Knight's Quest

Dinner Party Seating Puzzle

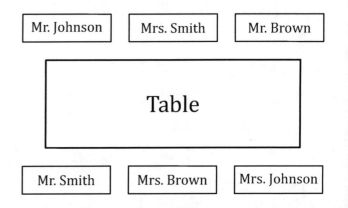

| Mr. Johnson | Mrs. Smith | Mr. Brown |

Table

| Mr. Smith | Mrs. Brown | Mrs. Johnson |

Adventure Word Search

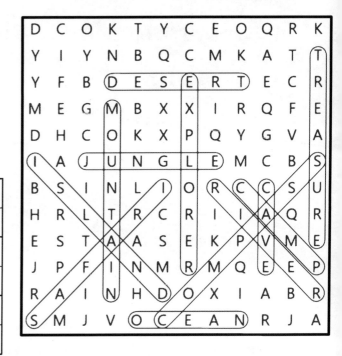

Sudoku #1

Medium 1

6	5	3	2	4	1
2	4	1	3	6	5
4	3	5	1	2	6
1	2	6	4	5	3
3	6	4	5	1	2
5	1	2	6	3	4

Medium 2

5	3	1	6	2	4
6	2	4	5	1	3
2	6	3	1	4	5
4	1	5	3	6	2
1	5	2	4	3	6
3	4	6	2	5	1

Medium 3

1	2	4	6	3	5
6	5	3	4	1	2
5	4	6	1	2	3
3	1	2	5	6	4
4	3	1	2	5	6
2	6	5	3	4	1

Medium 4

2	3	1	4	6	5
5	4	6	2	1	3
3	2	4	6	5	1
1	6	5	3	2	4
4	1	2	5	3	6
6	5	3	1	4	2

Jokes Decoding #2

Q: What kind of fish is the most valuable?
A: Goldfish!
Q: How do the oceans say hello to each other?
A: They wave
Q: What do you call a golden retriever at the beach?
A: A hot dog!
Q: Where do sharks go on vacation?
A: Finland!

Mixed Up Crowns

	Red	Blue	Green	Yellow	Purple
George	X	X	X	O	X
Henry	X	O	X	X	X
Richard	O	X	X	X	X
Louis	X	X	X	X	O
John	X	X	O	X	X

Word Ladder Adventure #2

GAME

GALE

BALE

BALL

BELL

BELT

MELT

Space Crosswords

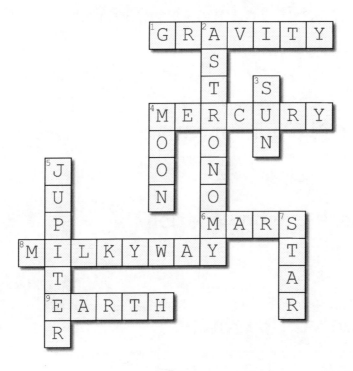

Arrange the Cars

| YELLOW | RED | GRAY | GREEN | BLUE |

Find the Spaceship

Guess the Fashion Brand #2

1. Chanel
2. Prada

Sudoku #2

Medium 5

6	4	5	3	1	2
1	3	2	6	5	4
2	1	4	5	3	6
5	6	3	4	2	1
3	2	6	1	4	5
4	5	1	2	6	3

Medium 6

5	3	1	4	6	2
2	6	4	5	1	3
1	2	6	3	5	4
3	4	5	1	2	6
4	1	2	6	3	5
6	5	3	2	4	1

Medium 7

2	5	1	3	4	6
6	4	3	1	2	5
4	3	2	6	5	1
5	1	6	4	3	2
3	6	5	2	1	4
1	2	4	5	6	3

Medium 8

3	6	1	2	5	4
5	2	4	3	6	1
6	1	2	5	4	3
4	3	5	6	1	2
1	5	3	4	2	6
2	4	6	1	3	5

Animals Word Search

```
T  P  E  T  K  A  N  G  A  R  O  O
D  W  G  M  S  N  R  Z  U  I  G  N
J  O  P  D  Y  S  Y  Z  C  D  J  I
A  U  L  E  O  P  A  R  D  Y  F  F
H  W  K  P  E  N  G  U  I  N  E  L
L  X  O  H  H  G  O  R  I  L  L  A
J  T  A  Q  T  I  G  E  R  J  E  M
V  F  L  T  A  R  N  O  G  K  P  I
C  P  A  N  D  A  Z  M  J  A  H  N
I  T  J  J  U  F  M  B  K  O  A  G
G  R  U  I  K  F  C  I  K  Y  N  O
D  Q  Z  T  Z  E  B  R  A  D  T  M
```

Jokes Decoding #3

Q: What did the bored goat say?

A: Mehhh!

Q: What does a dinosaur call a porcupine?

A: A toothbrush!

Q: What's as big as a dinosaur but weighs nothing?

A: Its shadow!

Q: What did the little corn say to the mama corn?

A: Where is pop corn?

Who Sits Where?

Jhon

Emma

Lily

Table

Rachel

Sam

Roger

Space Crosswords

Crossword grid:
- 1 Down: CREAMING
- 2 Across: GLUTEN
- 3 Down: CAKETIN
- 4 Down: TRUFFLES
- 5 Across: BAKINGPOWDER
- 6 Down: SPATULL
- 7 Across: FOAM
- 8 Across: WHISK
- 9 Across: VANILLA
- 10 Across: YEAST

Monster Friends

54 x 5 =

37 x 3 =

85 x 7 =

53 x 9 =

26 x 6 =

86 x 9 =

48 x 2 =

27 x 7 =

87 x 3 =

79 x 5 =

37 x 8 =

88 x 7 =

75 x 6 =

64 x 4 =

98 x 3 =

96 x 5 =

47 x 9 =

Guess the Fashion Brand #3

1. Louis Vuitton
2. Ralph Lauren

Shopping Adventure Puzzle

Name	Money	Bought
Sam	$3.00	Candy
Jack	$10.00	Game
Jm	$5.00	Book
Sarah	$8.00	TOY

Word Ladder Adventure #3

HUGE

LUGE

LURE

CURE

CARE

CARS

EARS

Melody's Coloring Challenge

Red	Green	Yellow
Red	Green	Green
Yellow	Red	Yellow

Spooky Cemetery Maze!

Fantasy Word Search

```
C A Y J G V X E K W X V
J A T H F G O B L I N V
L K B E A A N M N Z G R
K T L B N K I E K A V E
B B O V F C O R N R Q S
L L Z J H H M Y D M C
Z H L D P B M A J K E Y
L A G R I F F I N L L P
F X E A L N I D T T F U
K N I G H T H S M X E C
I U R O P M A G I C P D
N W U N I C O R N T Y Q
```

Sudoku #3

Hard 1

3	6	4	5	1	2
1	5	2	4	6	3
2	4	6	3	5	1
5	1	3	2	4	6
4	2	1	6	3	5
6	3	5	1	2	4

Hard 2

4	1	5	3	6	2
2	3	6	4	5	1
1	6	3	2	4	5
5	4	2	1	3	6
3	5	1	6	2	4
6	2	4	5	1	3

Hard 3

3	1	5	6	2	4
2	6	4	3	5	1
4	3	6	2	1	5
5	2	1	4	3	6
1	4	2	5	6	3
6	5	3	1	4	2

Hard 4

6	3	1	2	5	4
4	5	2	6	1	3
5	4	6	3	2	1
2	1	3	4	6	5
3	6	5	1	4	2
1	2	4	5	3	6

Pyramid Addition

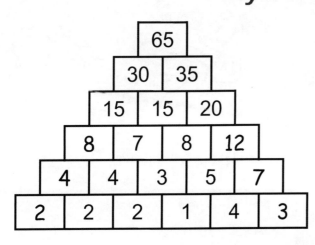

Pyramid 1:
- 65
- 30, 35
- 15, 15, 20
- 8, 7, 8, 12
- 4, 4, 3, 5, 7
- 2, 2, 2, 1, 4, 3

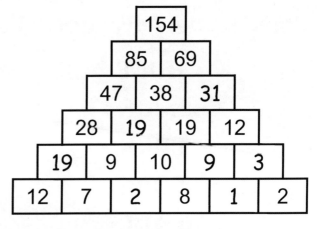

Pyramid 2:
- 154
- 85, 69
- 47, 38, 31
- 28, 19, 19, 12
- 19, 9, 10, 9, 3
- 12, 7, 2, 8, 1, 2

Number Arrow Challenge

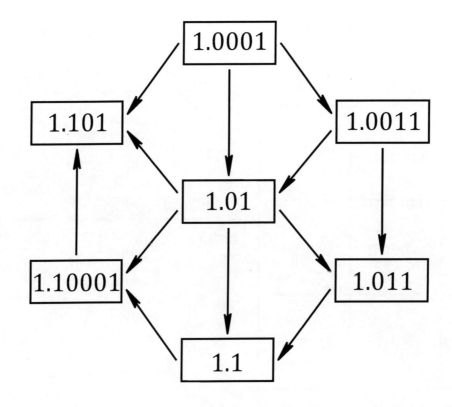

1.0001, 1.101, 1.0011, 1.01, 1.10001, 1.011, 1.1

Grandma's Jam Jars

There are three possible solutions

	Small Jar	Medium Jar	Large Jar
Solution 1	Blueberry	Peach	Raspberry
Solution 2	Blueberry	Raspberry	Peach
Solution 3	Raspberry	Blueberry	Peach

Scissor Search

Guess the Fashion Brand #4

1. Burberry
2. Nike

Insects Crosswords

Food Word Search

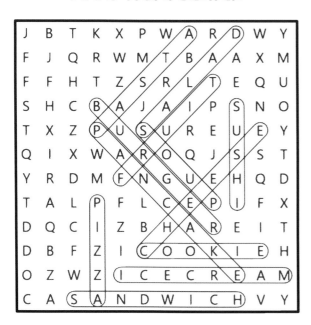

Thank you for getting our activity book for your amazing girl!

We hope she had a blast completing the activities and that the book added a touch of fun and creativity to her day.

If you have a moment, we would love it if you could leave a review on Amazon. Your feedback helps other parents decide if the book is right for their children, and it helps us improve and reach more families in need of educational and entertaining resources. Plus, it's always wonderful to hear what you think of our work!

Thank you in advance for your help, and we hope you and your child have an awesome day!

Kindest regards,

Creative Funland

Made in the USA
Monee, IL
02 December 2024